Big Bug

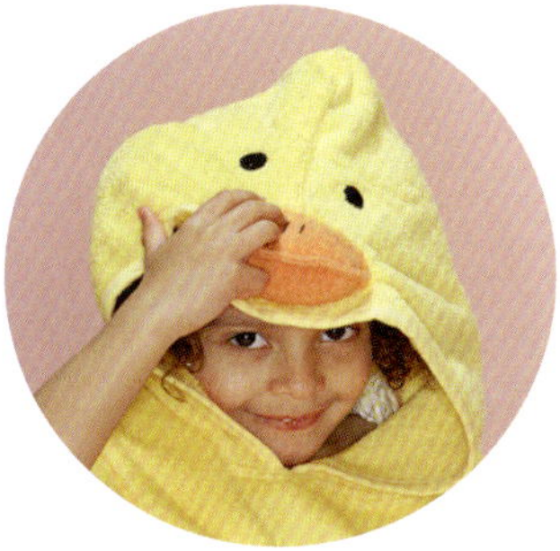

Written by
Stephen Rickard

Ransom

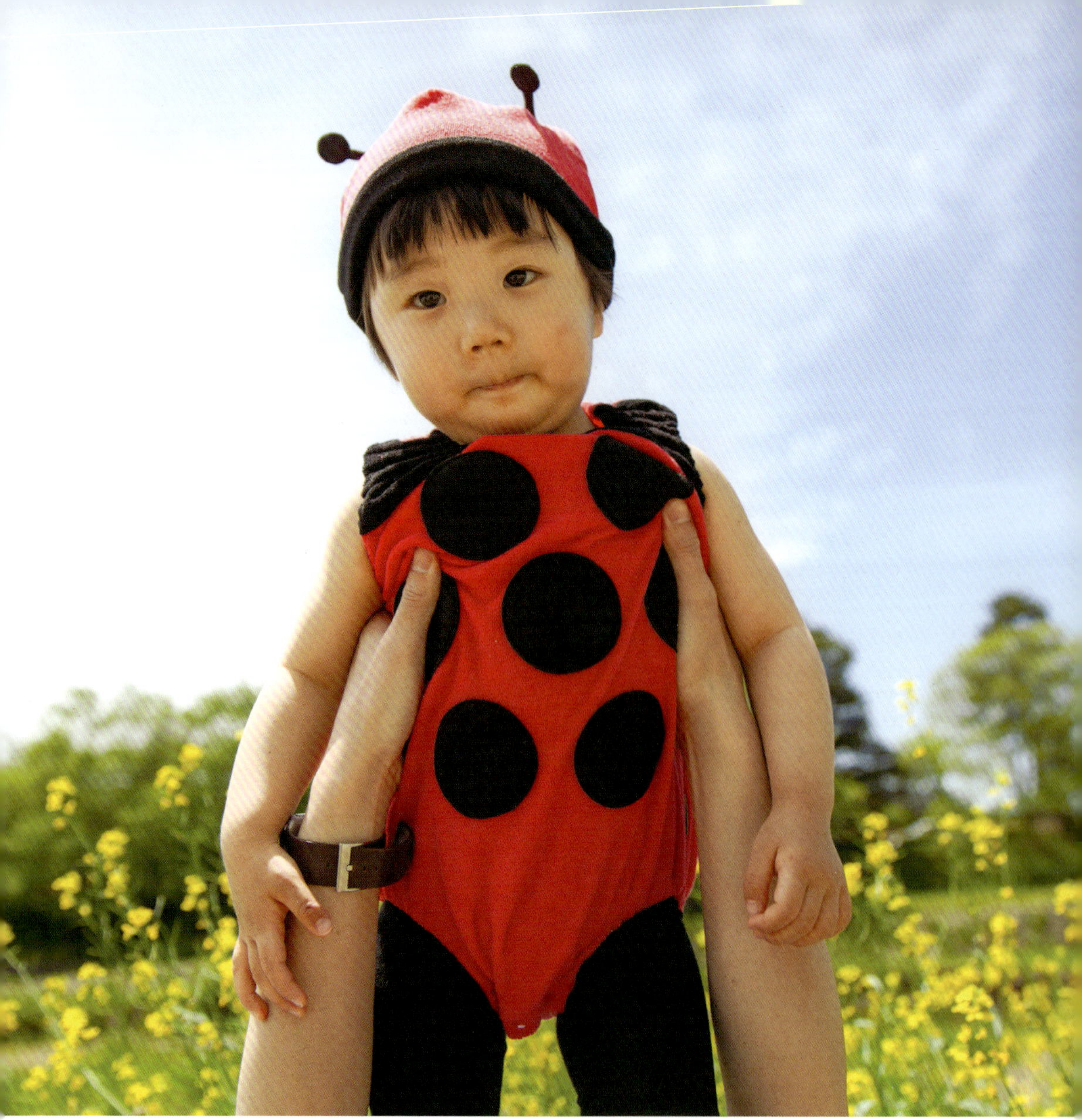

I am a big bug.

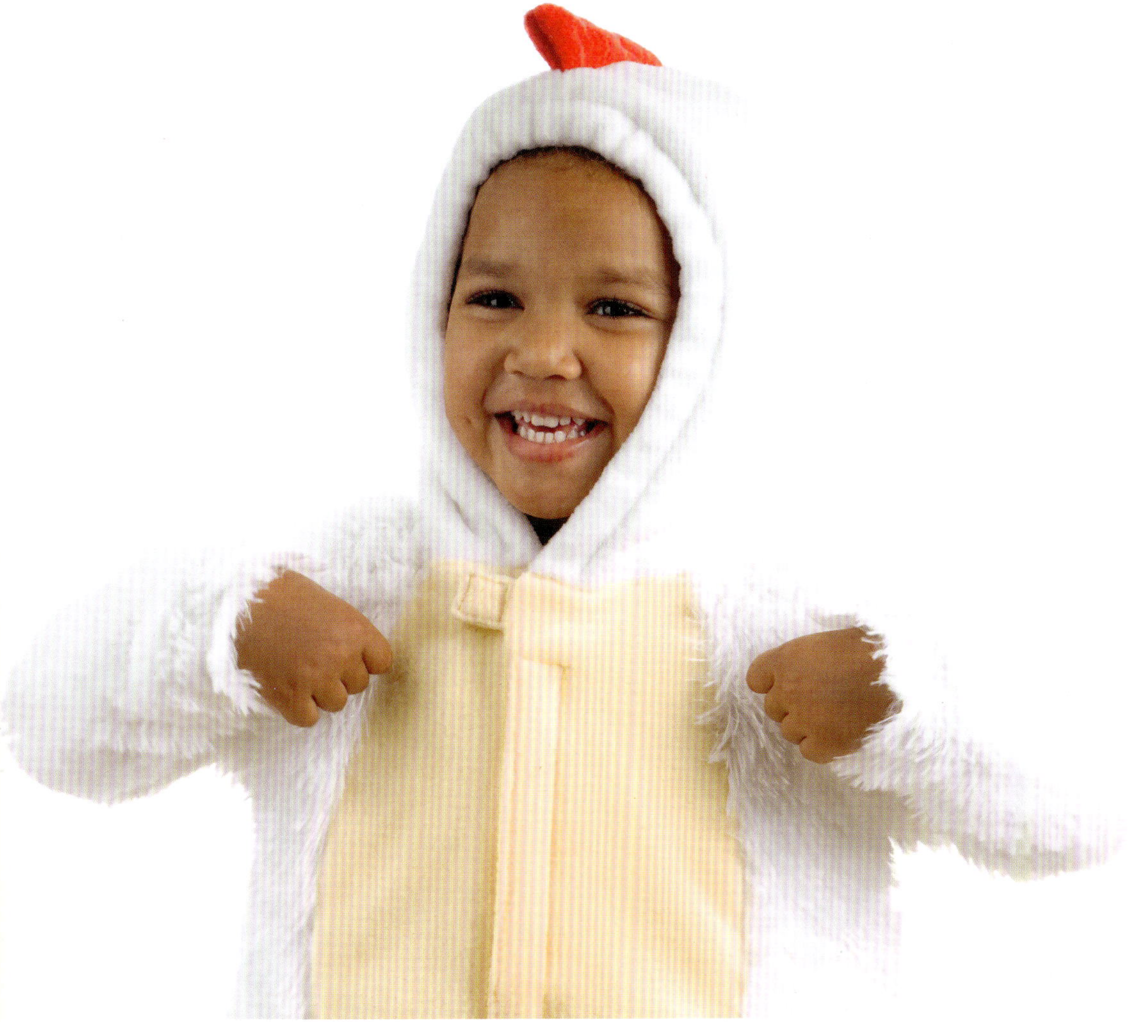

I am a big hen.

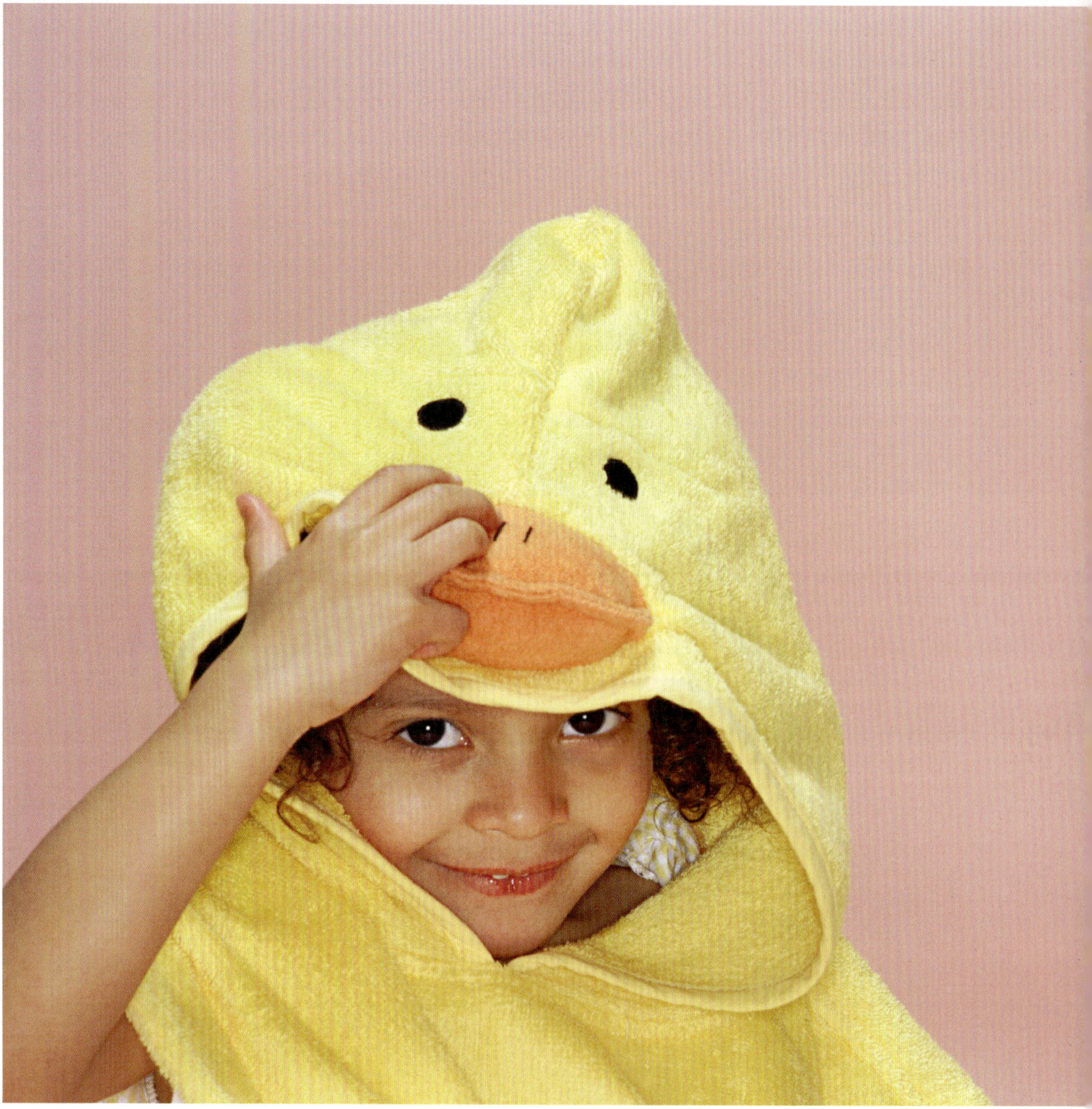

I am a big duck.

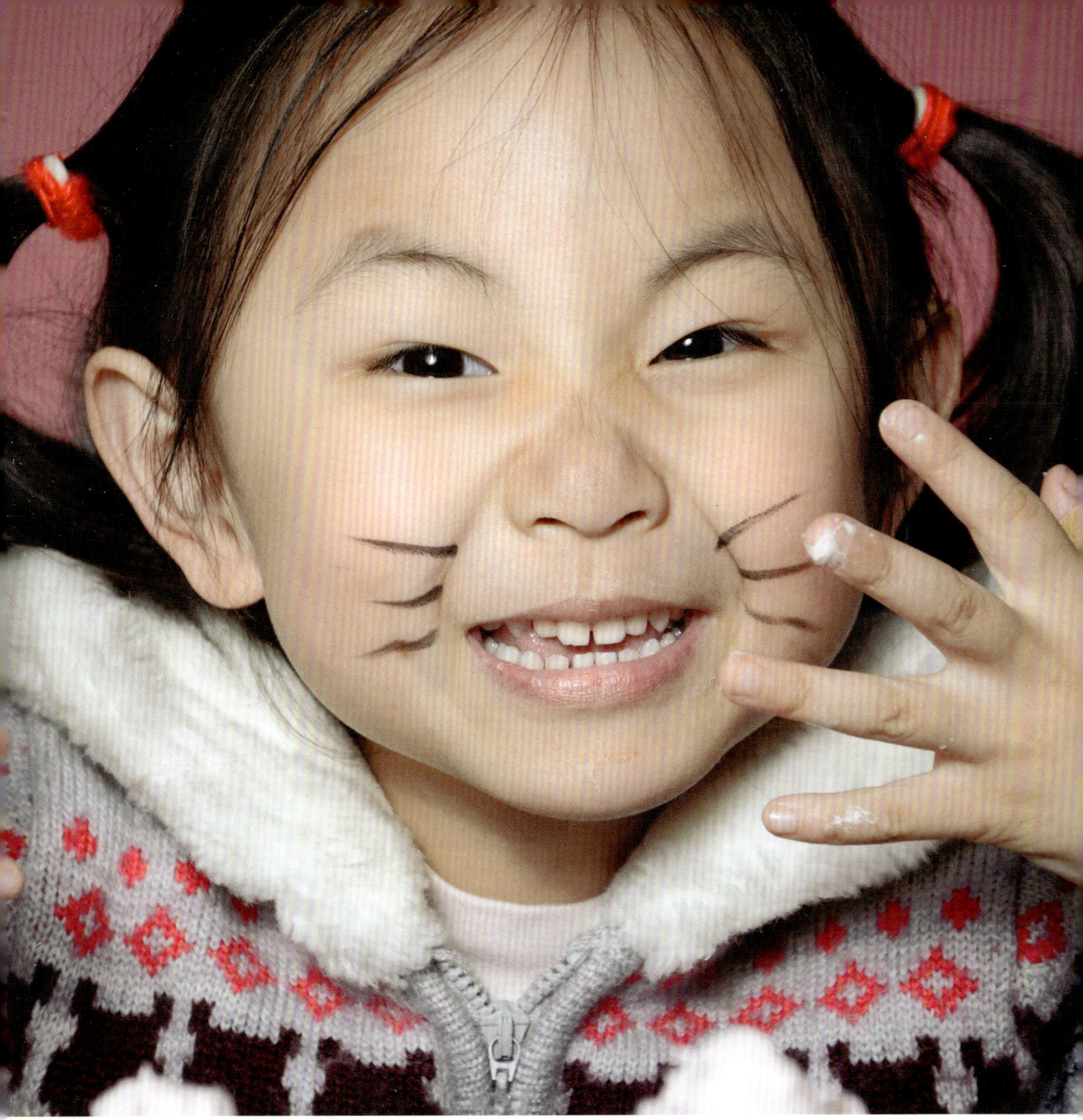

I am a big cat.

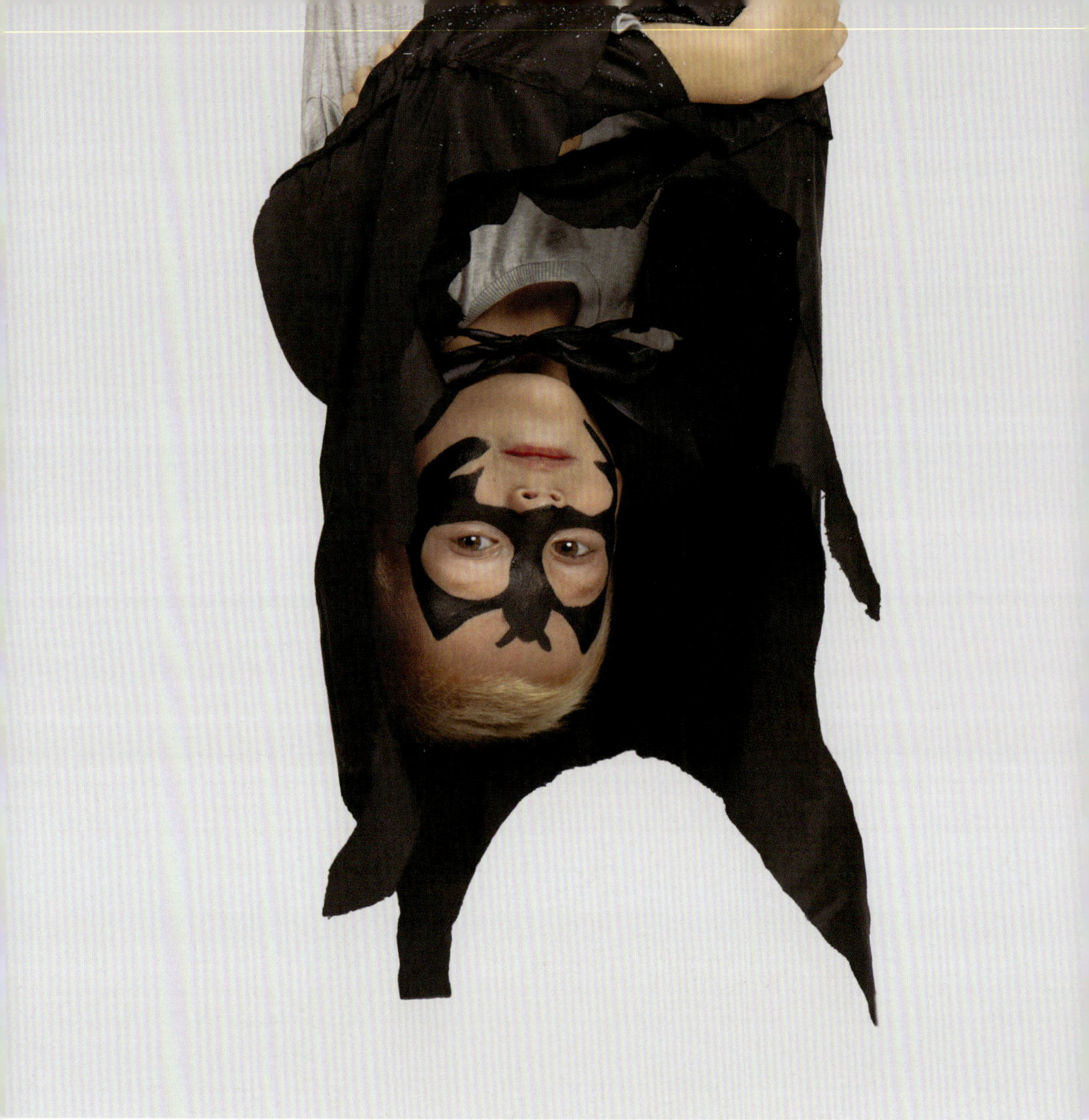

I am a big bat.

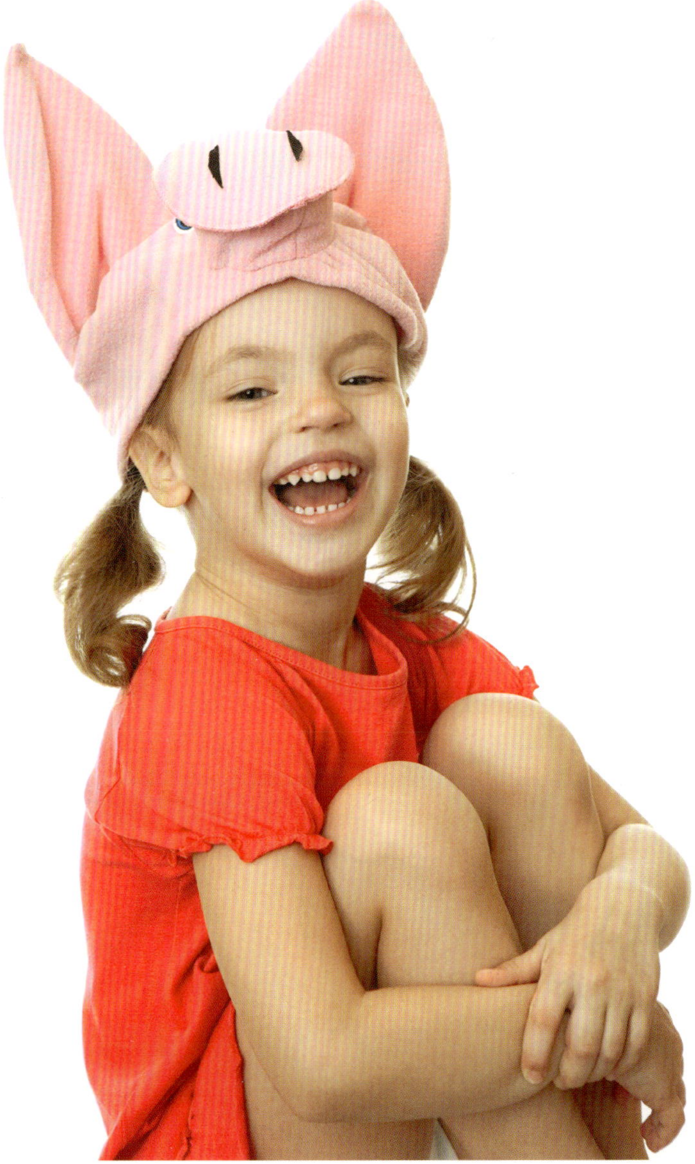

I am a big pig.

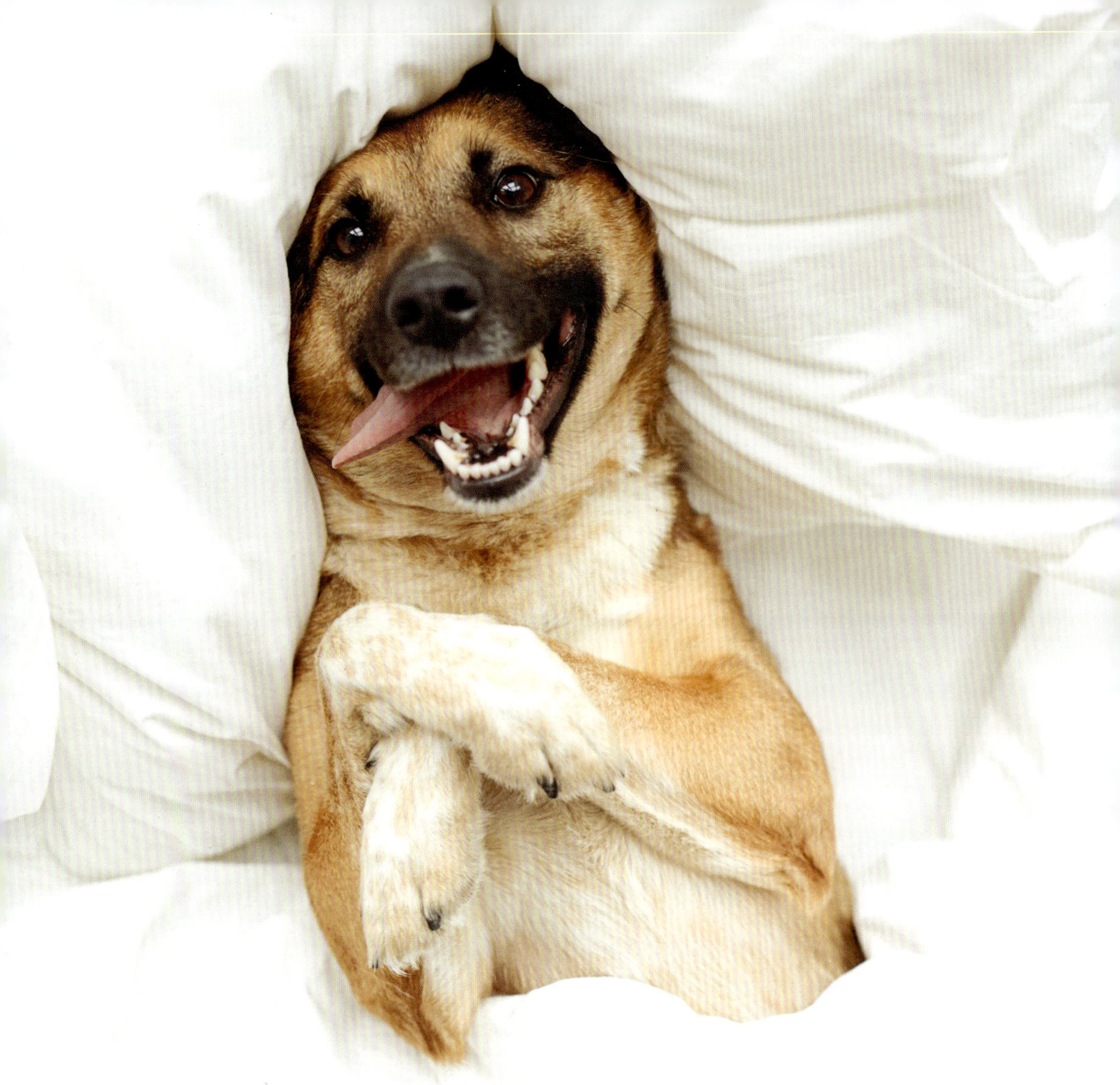

I am a big dog.

Ruff! Ruff!